DEDICATION

For my daughter, my mom, my sister, my nieces, and every single one of my girlfriends. For every woman I have had the privilege of mentoring, coaching or praying with. Your story is epic. God has a plan for your life and He can't wait for you to get on board!

CONTENTS

ACKNOWLEDGMENTS

Father God, thank you for loving me like you do.
Jesus, thank you for your sacrifice.
Holy Spirit, thank you for leading me.

Week One – Tamar
Breaking out of convention

DAY ONE
MY TAKE ON TAMAR

Are you ready to read about the five women who
started it all? The five women God chose to place
in the HIStory books? He put them there for a
reason. It is not coincidental. Nothing He does is
ever coincidental. Do you think you cannot be used
by Him? Do you think that your past, your gender,
your upbringing, your age, your education
somehow disqualifies you from serving Him? I have
a feeling that by the time we are done with this
study you will feel differently. I have a feeling that
when you meet these women you will realize that
God Himself created you with great purpose. So
buckle up.

As much as I would love to present to you flowery
love stories from the Bible...like the fairy tales we
read as children. I can't. They are just not realistic.
The truth is that women were not valued and not
regarded at all back then. We really have come a
long way...baby. And it was a hard-fought battle.
Too hard and too costly for us to live our lives as
though it didn't happen. It happened. Thank God it
happened. Thank God there were women who
stepped up to be all that God had created them to
be, so that you and I can stand up today and step
into all God has called us to be.

And...while I'm at it...I don't want you to think that
we can ONLY learn from the women in the Bible.

3

Some of my favorite people in the Bible are not women. Some of the people in the Bible I most relate to are men. But it is important that, as women, we look at the women and who they were...what they did. This study, this look into the Bible, will just focus on women. If you are a guy, welcome. Join us as we look at where we've come from. We are all brothers and sisters in Christ. We are all highly valued and loved by the King. So, I'm not trying to ignore you, but I am trying to call women out and up. So, let's take a quick look at Tamar.

Let's start with a little bit of back story. Judah was the brother of Joseph, you know, the one sold into slavery by his brothers? Yeah, him. At some point Judah decided to leave his brothers, move away, and marry a Canaanite woman named Shua. They were not supposed to marry women from Canaan. But he did. He and his wife had three sons. The oldest son was Er. When Er was of age, Judah and Shua found a wife for him. Her name was Tamar. Unfortunately, Er was not a good guy. He "did evil in the sight of God'. So, God killed him. As was tradition for that culture, the brother of the deceased was to have a child with the widow so she would have a secure future in the family. Why? Because only the men could inherit the family wealth and property. Without a son she would be destitute. So, she needed to have one. As was customary, Judah told his second son to marry Tamar and help her have a son. He did have sex with her, but purposely "spilled his seed" so she would not get pregnant. If she had a child that child would take part of the inheritance. I mean that was the point, right? But he was a little greedy and didn't want to share. He didn't really care about Tamar's future. Well, that seriously displeased God, and God killed him too.

Whew, aren't you glad we have Jesus as our mediator? I know I am!

Anyway, at that point Judah was afraid that if his youngest son married Tamar he would die too. Judah made an assumption that the problem was the woman (Tamar) and not his evil sons. So, he told Tamar to go back to her father's house as a widow and live there until his youngest son grew up. Only Judah had no intention of his youngest son marrying Tamar. So, years went by, the youngest son grew up, and Judah's wife died. Somewhere along the line Tamar realized that Judah was not about to make good on his duty. Tamar took matters into her own hands. She covered her face and pretended to be a prostitute and slept with her father-in-law...and got pregnant! She basically tricked him into fulfilling his duty with her and in doing so secured her own future financial status and position.

Have you ever felt as though your entire future was dependent on someone else? Maybe a spouse, or a specific job? Did that make you feel completely out of control of your own life? Perhaps you feel as though a lack of education has put limits on how far you can go. Or maybe your family upbringing has convinced you that you can't do more. You are only as stuck as you allow yourself to be. I know that sounds like a self-help pep talk, but it's not. I really do believe that I can do all things through Christ who strengthens me. I really do believe that if He calls me to it no one can take it from me. But I haven't always felt that way. I'm sure you have struggled with that as well. Maybe you are struggling with it right now. In the book of Romans we see these two things:

1. If God is for us who can be against us
2. In all these things we are more than conquerors

But oftentimes our experiences and the opinions of others lead us to believe that we are limited. It's time to remove those limits. It's time to start believing what the Bible says about us.

Today I want you to read the scriptures for this story. There's so much more in there that I didn't tell in the general overview above. We are going to dig into it more throughout the week. Wrong choices, not trusting God, choosing to act on what is right. As is true with every story in the Bible, we can learn valuable lessons from Tamar and her family. Let's pray for God to open our understanding as we read.

PRAY
God, as I read this story and study it throughout the week, will you open my eyes and ears to Your truth. Will you help me learn from the timeless truths of Your Word and show me who I am? In Jesus' name, amen.

READ
Read the story of Tamar in Genesis 38

JOURNAL

As you read the story of Tamar today take notes on the following journal page to record your initial thoughts.

Journal Page

_____

_____

_____

_____

_____

_____

_____

_____

_____

_____

_____

_____

_____

_____

_____

_____

_____

_____

_____

_____

_____

_____

TAMAR DAY TWO
FAITH TAKES ACTION

Did you read the scriptures yesterday? I'm sure you have a little more insight into why in the world Tamar would pretend to be a prostitute and sleep with her father-in-law. Because I'm sure that's nothing any of us would ever imagine doing. Not in our day, not in our story. But in hers….in hers we could see it.

There she was, still in her mourning clothes….all those years later. She was stuck in limbo. Placed there by her father in law...unfairly. She couldn't remarry, she couldn't have children, she had no future, no hope. But at some point she came to a place where that was no longer good enough for her. She wanted what was rightfully hers. What was rightfully hers? A future that was financially secure. A position in the family of Judah. Children.

There's a scripture in James 2 that might help clear this up a little.

> **14**What good is it, my brothers, if someone claims to have faith, but has no deeds? Can such faith save him? **15**Suppose a brother or sister is without clothes and daily food. **16**If one of you tells him, "Go in peace; stay warm and well fed," but does not provide for his physical needs, what good is that? **17**So too, faith by itself, if it is not complemented by action, is dead.

18But someone will say, "You have faith and I have deeds." Show me your faith without deeds, and I will show you my faith by my deeds. **19**You believe that God is one. Good for you! Even the demons believe that—and shudder.

20O foolish man, do you want evidence that faith without deeds is worthless? **21**Was not our father Abraham justified by what he did when he offered his son Isaac on the altar? **22**You see that his faith was working with his actions, and his faith was perfected by what he did. **23**And the Scripture was fulfilled that says, "Abraham believed God, and it was credited to him as righteousness," and he was called a friend of God. **24**As you can see, a man is justified by his deeds and not by faith alone.

25In the same way, was not even Rahab the prostitute justified by her actions when she welcomed the spies and sent them off on another route? **26**As the body without the spirit is dead, so faith without deeds is dead.

Clear as mud? Okay, see, without work (or action) faith is dead. She could have spent the rest of her life in her father's house having faith that Judah would do what was right. But she couldn't control him. She couldn't make him do the right thing. She could believe all day long, but if she didn't act on it nothing was ever going to change.

Now, the way she acted on it doesn't make much sense to us in our culture. But in their culture, it did. Our laws are different today. Women have position and value in our culture. So, there would never be a need to do what she did. But there will most definitely be a need for us to act in faith in likely every single situation. It's up to us to seek God and ask Him what He wants us to do. It's up to us to read the Word and find out how we are to act. And then it is up to us to move. It's up to us to act. It's up to us to go. The story may not turn out exactly as we would have hoped. But when we trust God, pray, and take steps we see Him leading us in, He will lead us into His plan. He does have a plan for you. And that plan is good.

Tamar was tired of living a life of less than. She was tired of living where God did not call her to be. She was ready to receive what was rightfully hers. What is rightfully yours? An abundant life. Peace. Grace. Joy. Tamar was ready to lose the mourning clothes and step into joy.

Is there something you have been mourning? The death of a loved one? The loss of a relationship, a job, a dream? It's time to lose the mourning clothes. It's time to accept that you cannot control that thing. You cannot change what was. But you can change what is to come. You can choose to seek God's plan and will for your life and live in all He has called you to.

PRAY

Lord Jesus, I know You have a plan for me. I know You have good things for me. I am tired of mourning the past, I am ready to live in the present and step into the future. Thank You for calling me up and out. Thank you for Your Word. Today I choose to follow You into all you have planned for me, In Jesus name, amen.

TAMAR DAY THREE
BLESSED

After all we have read about Tamar the last two days, blessed isn't exactly the word most of us would use to describe her. We actually might label her as more of a black widow. Or perhaps unfortunate. Cursed? Mistreated? A loser? I'm sure we could come up with many different ways to describe Tamar, but blessed would not be one of them. Yet, that's exactly how she was regarded in the Bible. Check out Ruth 4:12

> Through the offspring the LORD gives you by this young woman, may your family be like that of Perez, whom Tamar bore to Judah."

This statement was a blessing, not a curse. It was spoken over Boaz and meant to bless him and his family. Tamar was considered blessed and in turn her son Perez was blessed as well.

In the middle of the situation no one would have considered Tamar blessed. In fact, they all felt sorry for her. They knew she had been wronged by Judah, but their knowing didn't change her situation. She was still alone. She was still going to be poor for the rest of her life. They didn't know the blessing that was out ahead of her. Actually, she didn't either. And isn't that just like us? We worry and fret over what God is going to do. We feel defeated and wring our hands trying to think of a way out. But God already has a plan. And we know that His plans are good. So why do we not just trust Him?

I remember when my husband took a job in Texas almost ten years ago now. Many of our friends and family thought he was crazy...thought we were crazy. But we really believed God was leading us. It didn't look right from the outside. He had a good job at a local municipality. It paid well enough, and he could work overtime. He would be a fool to leave his job for something uncertain. But we took the step of faith. He was only in that position for a short time. He took a couple of transfers that led us back to Michigan, and has been promoted within his organization. Today he is making twice as much as he did back then. Not only that, back then his work was very physically taxing. Today he is in management, so it is far less taxing. But where would we be if he had chosen to listen to the fear inside of him, or the words coming at him from others? He would be right where he was ten years ago. But way more tired.

What if Tamar listened to the voices inside of her telling her not to do what she was going to do? What if she listened to Judah who said she would never be anything more than a widow not fit for marriage? She stepped outside of the thoughts and words and stepped into the unknown. She took a chance and secured her future. And Judah himself called her more honorable than he. Remember? When she finally was able to reveal that she was pregnant by him, look:

> **26**Judah recognized the items and said, "She is more righteous than I, since I did not give her to my son Shelah." And he did not have

14

relations with her again.

And at the end of this portion of scripture, just at the close of this story, we see one final indicator of just how blessed Tamar was. She had twins! A double blessing. Both of them were boys. She went from no hope of ever having children to having two sons. Her future was secure.

Many times God is calling us into something that looks hopeless. We can't see the double blessing on the other side of our faith. We have to trust Him and act on that trust in order to birth His plan in our lives.

PRAY

Lord, I want the double blessing You have planned for my life. I want to trust and birth Your plan for my life. Help me to shut out every voice that is not of You. Help me to clearly hear and see You and Your direction. In Jesus name, amen.

TAMAR DAY FOUR
WISDOM VS. EMOTION

At this point we just have to admit that Tamar was pretty sharp. She flawlessly pulled off what has to be the greatest trick of all time. Her own life was at risk in the middle of it. Yet she seemingly never batted an eyelash. First, she pretended to be a prostitute, then she cleverly asked for proof that she was with Judah!

15When Judah saw her, he thought she was a prostitute because she had covered her face. **16**Not realizing that she was his daughter-in-law, he went over to her and said, "Come now, let me sleep with you."

"What will you give me for sleeping with you?" she asked.

17"I will send you a young goat from my flock," Judah answered.

But she replied, "Only if you leave me something as a pledge until you send it."

18"What pledge should I give you?" he asked.

She answered, "Your seal and your cord, and the staff in your hand." So he gave them to her and slept with her, and she became pregnant by him. **19**Then Tamar got up and departed. And she removed her veil and put on her widow's garments again.

20Now when Judah sent his friend Hirah the Adullamite with the young goat to collect the items he had left with the woman, he could not find her. **21**He asked the men of that place, "Where is the temple prostitute who was beside the road at Enaim?"

"No temple prostitute has been here," they answered.

22So Hirah returned to Judah and said, "I could not find her, and furthermore, the men of that place said, 'No temple prostitute has been here.'"

23"Let her keep the items," Judah replied. "Otherwise we will become a laughingstock. After all, I did send her this young goat, but you could not find her." **24**About three months later, Judah was told, "Your daughter-in-law Tamar has prostituted herself, and now she is pregnant."

"Bring her out!" Judah replied. "Let her be burned to death!"

She had the foresight to know that she would need that proof. She knew Judah was not going to act honorably on her behalf at first. He wanted her dead and gone. She also had the patience to wait it out. Man, I need that kind of patience right now in my life. I absolutely hate waiting. I want things resolved NOW. But she waited and planned.

25As she was being brought out, Tamar sent a message to her father-in-law: "I am pregnant by the man to whom these items belong." And she added, "Please examine them. Whose seal and cord and staff are these?"

26Judah recognized the items and said, "She is more righteous than I, since I did not give her to my son Shelah." And he did not have relations with her again.

And in the end her wisdom, patience, forethought, and planning paid off. She did not allow her emotions to rule her. I feel like we all need to read that again. She did not allow her emotions to rule her. Why do I so often allow my emotions to rule me? They can cause me to miss so much. Yet, I give in to them time and again. But Tamar didn't. I'm sure she was feeling a million different negative feelings. Grief, fear, insecurity. But she pushed them aside and executed her plan. Flawlessly. How are your emotions today? Are they ruling you? Mine actually have been pushing me around today. It's no coincidence that today is the day I'm writing this. I needed to be reminded. And if you don't today, you will another day. Let's pray:

PRAY
Father God, will you show me how to not be ruled by my emotions? Will you help me stop and process things before I act? Will you teach me that while emotions are good, they should not run my life? In Jesus name, amen.

FIVE

TAMAR DAY FIVE
BREAKING BOUNDARIES

Wow. We have watched Tamar go from young wife to widow…twice. We have seen her unfairly sent away...for years. We have seen her risk her own life and end up winning. And ultimately being honored by being the first woman mentioned in the genealogy of Jesus.

1This is the record of the genealogy of Jesus Christ, the son of David, the son of Abraham:

> **2**Abraham was the father of Isaac,
> Isaac the father of Jacob,
> and Jacob the father of Judah and his brothers.
>
> **3**Judah was the father of Perez and Zerah by **Tamar**, (emphasis mine)
>
> Perez the father of Hezron,
> and Hezron the father of Ram.
> **4**Ram was the father of Amminadab,
> Amminadab the father of Nahshon,
> and Nahshon the father of Salmon.
> **5**Salmon was the father of Boaz by Rahab,
> Boaz the father of Obed by Ruth,
> Obed the father of Jesse,
> **6**and Jesse the father of David the king.

Not the kind of story we would have expected to see there. But the truth is right there in black and white. She really is the first woman listed in this genealogy. I know I have said this before, but it bears saying again. Women were not listed back then. Any one of Judah's children could have been in that list. That line could have gone a different way. But God chose Perez, son of Judah...son of Tamar.

Tamar started the whole thing. She was the first in a long line of women who lived outside of the box, who followed God...followed Jesus...changed our world. Will we do the same? Will we live outside of the box? Will we break out of the norms of convention and allow God to use us as He has planned?

Or will we shrink back and let the world (and often the church) tell us what we can and cannot do. Our instruction, our guard rails, our map, should come from only one place. They should come from God alone. He is our Savior, He is our Father, He gives us direction and He has a plan. I hope that Tamar has begun to open your eyes to the truth that we don't have to be perfect to be used by God. We don't have to fit a certain mold. We just have to love and trust Him. Are you ready to do that?

PRAY

Father God, after this week I am ready to trust in a deeper way. When I call you Father today, the words are weightier. They have more trust than ever before. You are my God and I trust You fully. In Jesus name, amen.

JOURNAL

As we wrap up the week on Tamar, use the journal page to record your thoughts.

Journal Page

_____

_____

_____

_____

_____

_____

_____

_____

_____

_____

_____

_____

_____

_____

_____

_____

_____

_____

_____

_____

_____

Week Two – Rahab
A woman of faith

DAY ONE
MY TAKE ON RAHAB

At first glance, when one looks at Rahab, they don't see what most would consider to be a woman of faith. They see her occupation. It tends to be one people don't easily forget. Rahab was a prostitute. Let's look at the scriptures in Joshua 2:1-3

> **1**And Joshua son of Nun secretly sent two spies from Shittim, saying, "Go, inspect the land, especially Jericho." So they went and entered the house of a prostitute named Rahab and stayed there.
>
> **2**And it was reported to the king of Jericho: "Behold, some men of Israel have come here tonight to spy out the land."
>
> **3**So the king of Jericho sent to Rahab and said, "Bring out the men who came to you and entered your house, for they have come to spy out the whole land."

What's happening here is that the Israelites have been in the wilderness for 40 years, Moses died, and they are about to go in and take the Promised Land. These two guys get sent to check it out before they go. There's this prostitute who lives in the wall of the city and they go to her place. The king was tipped off. So, someone close to Rahab told the king they were there. Here's Rahab, a prostitute with untrustworthy friends...in a less than ideal situation. We see in verses 4-8 that she hides the spies.

> **4**But the woman had taken the two men and hidden them. So she said, "Yes, the men did come to me, but I did not know where they had come from. **5**At dusk, when the gate was about to close, the men went out, and I do not know which way they went. Pursue them quickly, and you may catch them!" **6**(But Rahab had taken them up to the roof and hidden them among the stalks of flax that she had laid out there.)

> **7**So the king's men set out in pursuit of the spies along the road to the fords of the Jordan, and as soon as they had gone out, the gate was shut.

Then, this conversation follows in vs 8-11

> **8**Before the spies lay down for the night, Rahab went up on the roof **9**and said to them, "I know that the LORD has given you this land and that the fear of you has fallen on us, so that all who dwell in the land are melting in fear of you. **10**For we have heard how the LORD dried up

> the waters of the Red Sea*b* before
> you when you came out of Egypt,
> and what you did to Sihon and Og,
> the two kings of the Amorites across
> the Jordan, whom you devoted to
> destruction.**11**When we heard this,
> our hearts melted and everyone's
> courage failed because of you, for
> the LORD your God is God in the
> heavens above and on the earth
> below.

So, what happened? She heard, she believed, she proclaimed it to be true. She said, "I know," and then just a few words later she said, "the Lord". Did you catch that? Not your lord, or your god. No, she said, "The Lord". She believed. She had heard what was said about the God of Israel and she believed.

Let me just take you to a verse in John 20:29 really quick.

> Then Jesus told him, "Because you
> have seen me, you have believed;
> blessed are those who have not
> seen and yet have believed."

She wasn't there when He split the red Sea, but she had heard about it. She knew the truth when she heard it. Because she heard and believed she felt compelled to help the men of God. She simply had to. And as a result of that she was about to be ridiculously blessed.

Now, look at verse 11 again, what did she say? The Lord your God is God. She believed it to the point of risking her life on it...and the lives of her entire family! That is how much she knew who God was. That is how much she believed. Her faith was quite evident.

Maybe your story is a little cleaner than Rahab's. Maybe you have a difficult time seeing yourself in Rahab. But the truth is that we are all tainted. Romans 3:22 says:

> This righteousness is given through faith in Jesus Christ to all who believe. There is no difference between Jew and Gentile, for all have sinned and fallen short of the glory of God, and all are justified freely by his grace through the redemption that came by Christ Jesus.

So whether you told a lie, or have been a little loose with your sexuality, you have sinned and fallen short. But the good news is that Jesus came to redeem us. And just like Rahab, when we hear, believe and proclaim, we are accepted by Him...we too are added to the list of His family members.

As we study Rahab this week, let's put aside our preconceived ideas of who she was, and let's dig into who she became.

PRAY

Lord, would you open our hearts to Your Word today, as we read this story of Rahab and her faith, would you help us to see ourselves in Your bigger story? In Jesus' name, amen.

READ
Joshua 2 and Joshua 6

JOURNAL
As you read the story of Rahab today take notes on the following journal page to record your initial thoughts.

Journal Page

_____

_____

_____

_____

_____

_____

_____

_____

_____

_____

_____

_____

_____

_____

_____

_____

_____

_____

_____

_____

RAHAB DAY TWO
BOLDNESS

It would have been easy for Rahab to feel inferior, to not want to look at the men who came to her home. She would have surely been ashamed of what she had done. She was known by everyone as a prostitute. It was not at all a secret. But as we saw yesterday, she not only approached them, she boldly spoke what she came to understand as truth. That their God was actually THE God. And as a result she was not about to just let them leave. If they KNEW God, she wanted to be on their side. Check out the continuation of the story from yesterday, starting at verse 12.

> **12**Now therefore, please swear to me by the LORD that you will indeed show kindness to my family, because I showed kindness to you. Give me a sure sign **13**that you will spare the lives of my father and mother, my brothers and sisters, and all who belong to them, and that you will deliver us from death."

> **14**"Our lives for your lives!" the men agreed. "If you do not report our mission, we will show you kindness and faithfulness when the LORD gives us the land."

> **15**Then Rahab let them down by a rope through the window, since the house where she lived was built into the wall of the city. **16**"Go to the hill

country," she said, "so that your pursuers will not find you. Hide yourselves there for three days until they have returned; then go on your way."

17The men said to her, "We will not be bound by this oath you made us swear **18**unless, when we enter the land, you have tied this scarlet cord in the window through which you let us down, and unless you have brought your father and mother and brothers and all your family into your house. **19**If anyone goes out the door of your house into the street, his blood will be on his own head, and we will be innocent. But if a hand is laid on anyone with you in the house, his blood will be on our heads. **20**And if you report our mission, we will be released from the oath you made us swear."

21"Let it be as you say," she replied, and she sent them away. And when they had gone, she tied the scarlet cord in the window.

Did her family think she had finally lost it? Were they afraid she would be found out? Perhaps they had planned to pretend they didn't know. I'm sure deep inside they were hoping she was right, hoping it would all end up okay. When we are in those moments...where we can't see the other side of the situation...where we don't know how it will turn out...do we have the boldness to believe that God's Word is true?

When the negative report comes about our health, do we have the boldness to believe that by Jesus' stripes we were healed? When the negative financial report comes, do we have the boldness to believe that our God will supply all of our needs according to His riches in glory by Christ Jesus? Or do we run and hide in fear? Can we really believe that God will do what He says He will do? I know you've already read the end of Rahab's story, so you know these men did what they said. Do you know that God will be true to His Word for your life too?

It wasn't just words of faith in Rahab's case, she also acted in faith...in BIG ways. She hid the men, helped them escape, and then put a red cord outside of her window. She let them know her faith was solid. She let them know that she was expecting them to come back and do what they said they would. Acting like we believe is different than saying it. And it is also much more difficult. Sometimes the actions required are our own steps toward the right thing, so that God can help us through it. For example, I asked if you can believe God when the negative financial report comes. The steps you may need to take are first, repenting for mishandling your finances (unless of course it's a completely crazy, out of your control situation) and then speaking the Word of God out of your mouth over the situation. Then you have to do the right things to get your finances back in order. Things like, make a budget that fits your situation. Maybe you will have to cut some things out for a while.

Whatever those things are, do them while believing that God will be true to His Word.

Being a woman of faith takes boldness. If you don't have it, the good news is that you can develop it. You can ask God for it. You can read the scriptures and say them out loud to renew your own mind.

PRAY

Jesus, thank you for examples of boldness throughout Your Word. I know that sometimes I shrink back when I should step up. Would you help me to learn to trust more in You so that I too can be bold? Help me to know that You are there, You are leading me, and You are trustworthy. It's in Your name I pray, amen.

RAHAB DAY THREE
WHAT IS YOUR IDENTITY

We ended yesterday talking about Rahab's boldness, her choosing to help the Israelite men and then she tied a red cord outside of her window in faith that they would be true to their word.

So, then what happened??? The story goes on...

The Israelites took the Promised Land. They killed everyone in the city...except Rahab and her family. She ended up not only surviving but God chose to tell us about her...forever. Her story is written in His word as an example to us. An example of what? Of conviction, of courage, of wisdom, of boldness, and of faith. It doesn't sound like I'm talking about a prostitute with less than desirable friends, does it? But she wasn't defined by those things. Her past doesn't define her. We aren't given juicy details of what she once did. We are told her profession...I believe so we know that God uses everyone...and then we are told of her boldness and her faith. Once she believed, her story changed. Once she believed, she was a new person. She wasn't Rahab the prostitute anymore, she was Rahab the brave...Rahab the wise...Rahab the hero. I mean, to the men who she hid she was a hero. To her family, she was definitely a hero. They know what their fate would have been. She was made new.

We are also made new.

> Therefore, if anyone is in Christ, the new creation has come: The old has gone, the new is here!

2 Corinthians 5:17 NIV

As I read this story I wondered if she fought her own thoughts that day on the roof. Were her thoughts screaming at her, "You are a prostitute…these men are men of the living God! Who do you think you are??" But, somehow she pushed those thoughts down. Somehow, she managed to overcome her fear, her negativity, and choose to chase after freedom. She chose to no longer be defined by what she had done. She was going to be defined as something completely different moving forward. And she was. But it would not be easy. We can see in many different places in the Bible that she was called Rahab the harlot or Rahab the prostitute. Even when the men came back to save her family Joshua said in chapter 6 verse 22, "Go into the prostitutes house and bring her out and all who belong to her…" He didn't even use her name! But somewhere along the line she dropped the title. Somewhere along the line she stepped into what God called her to be. What is your title? Doctor? Teacher? Accountant? Mom? Wife? Or maybe your title is a little darker…Addict. Broke. Cheater.

The truth is that it doesn't matter who sees your title when they look at you. The truth is that you are not that at all. No, you are so very much more. You are a child of God. Yes, a child of God. He says you are. And, so, you are. Because when He speaks it is so. Like the time He said, "Let there be light", and there was.

We can see how people change in the presence of God. Look at Peter. He was with Jesus. His name was Simon. He was a fisherman. He swore and lied, and who knows what else. But Jesus changed his name to Peter - or Rock. Jesus knew that Peter would deny him. He knew that Peter would be afraid and try to run and hide. But he also knew who Peter really was. He also knew that Peter would be the leader of the New Testament church. So He called him what He knew he was. He does the same for us. He calls us the righteousness of God in Christ Jesus. He calls us His child, a joint heir with Christ. Because He knows who we really are, even when we don't.

PRAY

Lord, thank You for loving us even though we don't deserve it. Thank you for chasing us and telling us who we really are. God, would You give me a supernatural insight to know who I am in You? Would You help me to see me as You do, and in turn to see others as You do as well? In Jesus' name, amen.

FIVE

RAHAB DAY FOUR
SHAME

Have you ever read the names of God? He is
called things like Jehovah-Jireh (our provider) or
Jehovah-Rapha (our healer). That is who He is!
That is who He is to you! And you are called a joint
heir with Jesus. My gosh! How could that be? How
could I be a joint heir with Jesus?! How could He
love me at all?!

When I thought about Rahab standing there on the
roof, I wondered if her sense of shame felt heavy. I
talked yesterday about how I wondered if her
thoughts were screaming at her. I only wonder
because I've been there. When God has nudged
me to talk to someone about Him, and my mind
said, "Yeah right...you have no seminary education,
you can't do that!" Or when the attack has been a
little more personal. When I have felt the calling of
God to lead worship or to speak publicly about
Jesus, and the enemy whispers, "Don't you
remember where you've come from?" "Don't you
remember what you did." He would love nothing
more than to make me shrink back in shame and
stop myself from fulfilling God's plan for my life.

Surely Rahab had those moments too. Of course
this is speculation, but I can just see her there, at
her home, the prostitute. Men knock on the door
and she opens it, surely thinking they were there for
her. How her demeanor must have changed when
she began to realize who they were. I wonder if she
grabbed a shawl and wrapped it around her bare
shoulders. I wonder if she stepped out of the room
and wiped the lipstick off of her lips. I wonder. I

wonder if there was a fight in her mind. I almost don't have to wonder. I've been there enough to know for sure that there was. As the men spoke, her mind was racing. "I've heard of their God, I know He is really God!" "Now is my chance to know Him!", and undoubtedly in the next breath, "But how could He ever receive me, I'm unclean. In fact, I'm filthy". Yet, somehow she pushes through her shame to do what her spirit is telling her is the right thing. She chooses to look away from the mirror that yells her history and look at the window that holds her future.

Does shame talk to you? Does it remind you who you once were? Does it threaten to reveal who you really are? Ah...that's the one, isn't it. That's the one that makes you catch your breath. It has done it to me more times than I can count. "What if they find out who I really am?" It took me a long time to really understand that the old me is dead and gone. Buried with Christ. She would try to come back now and then, but I killed her. Sounds harsh, I know. But it had to be that way. So that I would know for sure. Now she is someone else's past. Mine is covered by the blood of Jesus. Yours is too. Shame has no hold on you. You are redeemed by the blood of the Lamb. He paid the price for you so you don't have to.

Just imagine you have a massive medical debt. Just massive. Like, let's say $200,000.00. And let's say the weight of that debt is hanging over you every single day. You get phone calls daily from the collection agency. So, you set up a payment plan. That plan straps you financially, but you have to do it. You work overtime and take all the money to the one you owe it to. You are tired, and worn out. But the interest keeps building and it seems as though the amount never goes down. Then one day you show up to pay your little measly payment, and you hear, "Oh, that debt has been paid in full." WHAT??? But how? Who? "Some man showed up and paid it off in cash, you don't owe us anything." Would you say to them, "But I want to pay that! It was my debt! I am the one who should pay for it!" No. You would leave that place shouting for the freedom of the weight that had been lifted from your life.

So why do we choose to continue to pick up the weight of shame and try to carry it ourselves? Why do we think we have to pay that debt when He paid it for us? When the enemy tries to remind you of who you once were, the sin you were once so steeped in, remind Him of what Jesus did. You have been set free from shame.

PRAY
Father, I am so sorry for trying to carry the debt You sent Your Son to pay. Thank you for paying it. Thank you for setting me free from bondage. Thank you for freeing me from guilt and shame. I choose today to let shame go and move forward trusting You. In Jesus' name, amen.

RAHAB DAY FIVE
RAHAB'S FUTURE

Are you feeling a little more free today? Like maybe you are no longer carrying the shame that you used to lug around in your bag? Have you come to know the story of Rahab a little better? Are you more comfortable with who she is? The story could end there, and we could probably be happy with it. Happy knowing that Rahab didn't allow her identity to be in what she did. Knowing that she didn't let her shame stop her from being rescued. The story could end here, in Joshua 6…

> **22**Meanwhile, Joshua told the two men who had spied out the land, "Go into the house of the prostitute and bring out the woman and all who are with her, just as you promised her." **23**So the young spies went in and brought out Rahab, her father and mother and brothers, and all who belonged to her. They brought out her whole family and settled them outside the camp of Israel.

> **24**Then the Israelites burned up the city and everything in it. However, they put the silver and gold and articles of bronze and iron into the treasury of the LORD's house. **25**And Joshua spared Rahab the prostitute, with her father's household and all who belonged to her, because she hid the men Joshua had sent to spy out Jericho.

> So she has lived among the
> Israelites to this day.

That sounds like a pretty good happily-ever-after doesn't it? Only it's not the end. There's a scripture in Isaiah 55:9 that says that God's thoughts and ways are higher than ours. And I'm so glad that they are! Whatever end we can think up, God can think up something far more incredible, far more amazing and awe-inspiring. And He did just that for Rahab.

We don't hear much more about Rahab in the Bible after this story in Joshua. There are a couple of reminders of her story in the New Testament.

> Hebrews 11:31 By faith the harlot
> Rahab perished not with them that
> believed not, when she had received
> the spies with peace.

> James 2:25 Likewise also was not
> Rahab the harlot justified by works,
> when she had received the
> messengers, and had sent them out
> another way?

Both of those accounts refer to her as a harlot (or prostitute). All that time later.

Oh yeah, there's one more. Really, the only one that counts…

> Matthew 1:1 starts out…
> The historical record of Jesus Christ,
> the Son of David, the Son of

Abraham:

Then it goes on to give the genealogy...Abraham fathered Isaac, who fathered Jacob, etc.

In verse 4 we read...
> Aram fathered Aminadab, who fathered Nahshon, who fathered Salmon, who fathered Boaz by Rahab.

Wait, what? Back up. Salmon fathered Boaz by whom? That's right, Rahab. The harlot? The prostitute? No, Rahab the mother of Boaz, in the lineage of Jesus. He renamed her, just like He did with Peter. Just like He has done with you. I can't even type it without getting choked up. He changed her name. He changed her identity. He listed her in the genealogy of the Savior of the World. My Lord, my Savior. She didn't have to be pure, because He was. We don't have to be pure, because He is...and He makes us pure in Him.

PRAY
Lord, it's hard to even form words that can express our gratitude for what You have done...for who You are. You love, and give, and forgive. Your grace is beyond anything we can imagine. Help us to not underestimate You. In Jesus' name, amen.

JOURNAL
As we wrap up the week on Rahab, use the journal page to record your thoughts.

Journal Page

_____

_____

_____

_____

_____

_____

_____

_____

_____

_____

_____

_____

_____

_____

_____

_____

_____

_____

_____

_____

Week Three - Ruth,
A Woman of Honor

DAY ONE
MY TAKE ON RUTH

Humble beginnings. We hear about them often, don't we? People are usually fascinated with people who come from poverty and overcome. Whether they start major corporations or become famous somehow...we want to know all about them. We all love a good comeback story. Well, have I got a good story for you. You may have already heard it, but probably when someone was talking about marriage. You have probably heard the name Boaz, and have probably been told to wait for your Boaz. Last week we learned about Boaz's mother, Rahab. But this week we are going to learn about a young, destitute woman named Ruth.

Ruth lived with her mother-in-law Naomi. Naomi was an Israelite woman. The Israelites were God's people. They worshiped the one true God. Naomi had been married to a man named Elimelek. They lived in a place called Bethlehem-Judah. Due to the Israelites disobedience to God, there was a famine in the land. Elimelek took Naomi, along with their two sons, to a place called Moab to protect them. Only the people in Moab did not worship the same God. In fact they worshiped a false God named Chemosh. Their family line could be traced back to Lot, but they broke off and no longer followed God.

Some years later Elimelek, Naomi's husband, died. Naomi's two sons married Moabite women - idol worshipers - women who did not worship God. Then, in a tragic twist, Naomi's two sons died, leaving both Ruth and Orpah widowed as well.

This would be devastating for anyone. But back in that time it was especially devastating. Women were not valued in that culture. So here they were, three widows, living together - they were outcasts. These women found themselves completely destitute. They owned nothing, they had nothing. No family, no jobs, they were destitute. The word destitute means "without basic necessities".

Perhaps some of us have been there. If we look at older meanings of the word, we find that it means "abandoned" or "empty". I'm pretty sure most of us have been there. We may be facing a situation in our life right now that has left us empty. We can surely relate to these women.

Naomi heard that God had answered the prayers of His people and ended the famine in Bethlehem-Judah, so she decided to go back home to her people and her God. She told her daughter's in law to go home to their parents in hopes they could remarry. But Ruth refused to leave Naomi. Look at the interaction between them:

Naomi said in Ruth 1:11-13:

> 11But Naomi replied, "Return home, my daughters. Why would you go with me? Are there still sons in my womb to become your husbands? 12Return home, my daughters. Go on, for I am too old to

have another husband. Even if I
thought there was hope for me to
have a husband tonight and to bear
sons, 13would you wait for them to
grow up? Would you refrain from
having husbands? No, my
daughters, it grieves me very much
for your sakes that the hand of the
LORD has gone out against me."
But Ruth replied in vs 16-17 "Don't
urge me to leave you or to turn back
from you. Where you go I will go,
and where you stay I will stay. Your
people will be my people and your
God my God. Where you die I will
die, and there I will be buried. May
the Lord deal with me, be it ever so
severely, if even death separates
you and me."

I think it can be easy to brush over this part of the
story, to think that Ruth was just supporting her
mother-in-law. But the truth is that there is a
conversion that took place here. I'm not sure if I
have ever heard anyone speak of Ruth's
conversion. If I did, I don't remember it. I just know
that one day, when I was reading, I saw it so
clearly. Ruth made a decision to leave her idols
and trust in God. She said, "your people will be my
people and your God my God." We then see her go
from calling Him "your God" to calling Him "my
Lord". She chose to become one of God's people. It
was a very real conversion. Very similar to the one
we saw last week in Rahab. Both of these women
saw or heard something and chose to believe it.

Ruth knowingly chose to go to a place where she didn't know anyone, she honored her mother-in-law, but most of all she honored God. In the depths of her despair, in the darkest times of her life, she chose God. I bet you can guess what happens in this story. I'm sure you already know that God blessed her. But the extent and depth of those blessings is mind blowing. We will dig further into the story this week and see if we can see a little bit of ourselves in Ruth.

PRAY

Father God, in moments of deep despair and loss, I can tend to pull back from You. I'm sorry for when I do. Will you help me choose You at those times? Will you help me choose to know that You are God? In Jesus' name, amen.

JOURNAL

As you read the story of Ruth today take notes on the following journal page to record your initial thoughts.

Journal Page

_____

_____

_____

_____

_____

_____

_____

_____

_____

_____

_____

_____

_____

_____

_____

_____

_____

_____

FIVE

RUTH DAY TWO
A HARD WORKER

Yesterday we left off with Ruth deciding to go with her mother-in-law to Bethlehem-Judah. It's important that you know that Naomi, Ruth's mother-in-law, was really struggling. She was depressed and negative, and who wouldn't be? She had just lost her husband and both of her sons. She had nothing. She showed up back in her hometown with her idol worshiping daughter-in-law hoping that somehow they'd find help. Ruth was faithful to Naomi. She stayed with her. When we learned about Rahab we learned that faith, believing in God, can make people do crazy, big, things. Rahab forsook the king to help the men of God and Ruth left her people to go with Ruth to her God. She had been converted and her life would never be the same.

They had arrived in Bethlehem-Judah at harvest time, and the people were harvesting grain in the fields. So, with approval from Naomi, Ruth decided to glean from what the harvesters were picking in order to provide for them. Gleaning is basically picking up the leftover grain and casings that drop on the ground.

Ruth asked permission of the manager of the field to glean there. So, she was following far behind the workers at this grain field and she basically picked up what was discarded and tried to find something valuable in it. I'm sure this was not glamorous work. I'm quite certain she was sweating, and likely afraid for her own safety. But someone had to provide for them. And she chose to go with Naomi, so she was going to do it.

The next thing we see is that the owner of the field showed up and asked his worker who the gleaner was. They said, "She's Ruth the Moabitess, Naomi's daughter in law". Naomi's people knew what Ruth had done for her. And this guy, Boaz, was so moved by her loyalty and commitment to Naomi that he decided to help her out. He doesn't regard the fact that she is an idol worshiper. We know she converted, but he didn't. The only thing the people there knew about her was that she was a Moabite woman. That's what they called her. Boaz told Ruth to continue to glean in his fields and promised to make sure she is safe. He then told his field manager to drop extra grain on the ground so Ruth would be sure to have enough. He even invited her to eat with his workers, and allowed her to take food back to her mother-in-law.

Who was this guy? He must have had money if he owned this business. And he obviously had compassion because he was moved by Ruth's situation. I have said this a million times, when we honor we will be honored. Maybe not by the person we are honoring. But we will be honored. Ruth honored Naomi, and she honored God by acknowledging Him as the one true God. Now she was reaping the rewards of that and God was using this man, Boaz, to meet her needs.

Honor is not always easy, but it is the right thing. Working hard is honorable. I think sometimes, in difficult situations, we may tend to think it is okay to do what may be considered less than honorable. We may think it's okay to bend the rules or stretch the truth or just flat out do the morally wrong thing. But the truth is that it is never okay. When we honor God by doing the right thing He will honor us. I've seen it time and again, and we see it here in this story of Ruth and her choice to work hard.

When Ruth got home that night Naomi asked her where she had been working because she brought so much food and grain home. When Ruth told her she was at the field of Boaz, Naomi said, "That man is our close relative, he is one of our guardian redeemers." In their culture the next of kin was supposed to take care of those who were widowed. And, as it turned out, Boaz was one of those relatives. It turns out, Ruth was in the right place at the right time.

As we continue to study this book this week, let's look for ways we too can be honorable in our daily life.

PRAY

God, there have been times when I have been less than honorable. Forgive me for those. Help me to choose honor, to choose the right thing. Help me to stay close to You. In Jesus' name, amen.

FIVE

RUTH DAY THREE
TEACHABLE

Ruth had so many characteristics that were good. She was indeed a good woman. Yesterday we learned that she was a hard worker. Today we are going to talk about how teachable Ruth was, and hopefully become a little more teachable ourselves.

One day Ruth's mother-in-law Naomi said to her in Ruth 3:1-4

> **1**One day Ruth's mother-in-law Naomi said to her, "My daughter, should I not seek a resting place for you, that it may be well with you? **2**Now is not Boaz, with whose servant girls you have been working, a relative of ours? In fact, tonight he is winnowing barley on the threshing floor. **3**Therefore wash yourself, put on perfume, and wear your best clothes. Go down to the threshing floor, but do not let the man know you are there until he has finished eating and drinking. **4**When he lies down, note the place where he lies. Then go in and uncover his feet, and lie down, and he will explain to you what you should do."

Weird, right? Not normal in our culture. But I assure you it was not sketchy in any way. In fact, our video today will talk about that. But right now, I want to focus on something different.

FIVE

So let's talk about Ruth for a moment. She was a younger woman and she could have gone back to her own family who did not believe in God and she could have found a husband there and started a new life but she saw Naomi, who she loved, choosing to run toward God. She saw Naomi in her pain saying 'God answered these people and I'm going there', and she chose to go with her. Ruth, in all of her pain - because she also lost her husband she also lost everything she was just as destitute as Naomi - she chose to believe in God. She chose to find Hope in a hopeless situation, and to also run toward God. She went to a place where she didn't know anyone, she chose to be honorable and to love and honor her mother-in-law, and she chose to work hard in the middle of a difficult situation. She said to herself 'I'm physically able and I'm going to do this', and she did. And as a result of her faith - of her trust - in both her mother-in-law and God, she found favor from someone who could alter her entire life.

And listen to how Ruth responded to Naomi in verse 5

> 5"I will do everything you say," Ruth answered. 6So she went down to the threshing floor and did everything her mother-in-law had instructed her to do.

There are times in our life when it's just us and God, when He is the only One we are to consult. But many times, He sends us people with godly wisdom to help us know what to do next. For Ruth, this was one of those times. But she had to be humble and open to receive instruction. Ruth had to be teachable. It can be really hard to be teachable. Often, when we need help the most, it seems we are most likely to not be teachable. But Ruth was open, and she was willing to do whatever Naomi said. She knew that Naomi knew God. She knew that Naomi had lived more life than she had, and had been through some stuff. She knew that she could trust Naomi. And her trust and humility paid off.

PRAY

Father God, I know I can be so stubborn. I know there are areas of my life where I have been closed off, unteachable. But I don't want that anymore, Lord. I want to be everything you have called me to be. I want all of Your plan for me. So, will You help me tear down those walls I have built up? Will You help me to be teachable? Will You send someone with Godly wisdom to help me? In Jesus name, amen.

FIVE

RUTH DAY FOUR
BE STILL

Ruth was teachable, we saw that clearly in our study yesterday. And thank God she was. Because her mother-in-law had a bit of advice for her that would benefit every one of us.

When Ruth returned from her nighttime meeting with Boaz, Naomi asked her what happened. Ruth proceeded to tell Naomi all about how honorable Boaz is, that he protected Ruth and promised to handle the situation. But he also told Ruth that there was another relative who was next in line as the guardian redeemer, and that he needed to allow him to choose whether or not he wanted the property...and Ruth. I have to believe that this made Ruth more than just a little nervous. She was in a strange place and the only people she knew were Ruth and Boaz. She didn't know who was safe and who was not. She had never even seen this man they were speaking of. She had no idea what kind of a man he was. He may have been horrible. I tend to believe that her voice gave all of those thoughts away as she spoke to her mother-in-law about her interaction with Boaz the night before. But Naomi's response to Ruth was filled with wisdom that can only come from years of experience.

Then, in Ruth 3:18, Naomi said,

> "Wait, my daughter, until you find out
> what happens. For the man will not
> rest until the matter is settled today."

Naomi knew Boaz, and she knew her God. She was certain it would all be okay. In her wisdom she was telling Ruth, don't try to figure this out, don't take unnecessary steps. Be still. Be patient, wait while God takes care of it.

I wish I had learned this lesson when I was young. Unfortunately, it has taken me 49 years! God doesn't need our help, He wants our obedience. So, sit still and let Him work it out. When He says move, move. When He says go, go. My own lack of patience or disregard for God has unfortunately led to many mistakes and wrong choices in my life. But what I've learned is this...His plan is always His plan. His purpose for your life doesn't change because you mess up, or because someone does something terrible to you. You may take a detour, but if you run back to Him and surrender, really surrender, He will take you back to the route that leads to your purpose. Yes, you'll miss some things if you get off of His original path, you'll face some things you were never meant to. But ultimately you will end up where He planned. It takes repentance and surrender. And a lot of obedience. So, if you have already messed up, don't panic. Repent, and get close to Him again. Let Him lead you again.

Be still and let Him lead. I know it's hard. I do. In fact, more than once I have literally purchased temporary tattoos that said, "Be Still" and put them on my wrist facing myself so I could be reminded over and over again to stop trying to handle it all myself. I am so, very glad I have finally learned this lesson. And it's still not easy, but I can walk myself through it and when I start to panic, I pray and speak the Word out of my mouth to bring myself back to "Be Still".

PRAY
Lord, I tend to try to fix things myself. I become restless and impatient. Help me to wait on You, to be still and wait for You to move. Will you move in my life today, Lord? In Jesus name, amen.

FIVE

RUTH DAY FIVE
THE FUTURE

This is our last day talking about Ruth. I hate for it to end. I just love her heart, her determination to do the right thing. I love her conversion and how God honors her. Let's look at where her life goes after that meeting with Boaz.

In chapter four Boaz does indeed go to the other relative. He tells him about everything, the property, Ruth. And he legally is allowed to marry Ruth as that relative chose to back out. So, Boaz does marry her, and the blessings poured out over both Naomi and Ruth as a result are laid out in history for all of us to see. Let's pick up in chapter 4, verse 13.

13So Boaz took Ruth and she became his wife. And when he had relations with her, the LORD enabled her to conceive, and she gave birth to a son.

14Then the women said to Naomi, "Blessed be the LORD, who has not left you this day without a kinsman-redeemer. May his name become famous in Israel. **15**He will renew your life and sustain you in your old age. For your daughter-in-law, who loves you and is better to you than seven sons, has given him birth."

16And Naomi took the child, placed him on her lap, and became a nurse to him. **17**The neighbor women said, "A son has been born to Naomi," and they named him Obed. He became the father of Jesse, the father of David.

Naomi took care of her grandson. The same women she told to call her bitter were calling her blessed. Ruth not only remarried and had a child, but she married a man who was highly regarded and successful. Both Ruth and Naomi had a future much greater than the past they lost.

Now read the rest starting in verse 18:

18Now these are the generations of Perez:

Perez was the father of Hezron,

19Hezron was the father of Ram,

Ram was the father of Amminadab,

20Amminadab was the father of Nahshon,

Nahshon was the father of Salmon,*c*

21Salmon was the father of Boaz,

Boaz was the father of Obed,

22Obed was the father of Jesse,

and Jesse was the father of David.

You are probably wondering why we are all of a sudden learning about Davids geneology. Here's why...Ruth was a gentile...not an Israelite...she was not a woman of God. But she became one. Though she wasn't born into it, she did choose it. And for all of their loss, all of their struggle...God chose to put Ruth and her son Obed in the lineage of Jesus Christ. Yes, Jesus comes from the line of King David. So, now Ruth and her baby Obed are forever documented in the genealogy of Christ. THAT is a comeback story if I've ever seen one!

It may look over to you, your future may look bleak to you, but so did Ruth's. She made simple, right choices and they led her straight into God's plan for her life.

Your future is out there, waiting to be had. Regardless of what today looks like. Step into it. It won't be easy, but it will be amazing.

PRAY
Lord, I am so blow away by Ruth's story, her comeback story. Why do I ever question You? Why do I ever think you won't do it for me too? Lord, thank you for how you are drawing me to You, how you are calling me to step into what You have called me to. I am choosing today to run after You. To decide to live this life as You have planned for me. In Jesus name, amen.

JOURNAL
As we wrap up the week on Ruth, use the journal page to record your thoughts.

Journal Page

_____

_____

_____

_____

_____

_____

_____

_____

_____

_____

_____

_____

_____

_____

_____

_____

_____

_____

_____

Week Four – Bathsheba
The QueenMother

DAY ONE
MY TAKE ON BATHSHEBA

The name Bathsheba conjures up various things for various people. Most people know her as the married woman who had an affair with King David. I've often wondered if she was just unfortunate, a woman in the wrong place at the wrong time. I've wondered if she was willing - maybe even excited to have gained the attention of the King, or if she was just scared and forced to do something she didn't want to. I mean, David was the King. Could she have said no? Let's look at the story of David and Bathsheba in 2 Samuel 11.

> **1**In the spring,*a* at the time when kings march out to war, David sent Joab with his servants and the whole army of Israel. They destroyed the Ammonites and besieged Rabbah, but David remained in Jerusalem.

> **2**One evening David got up from his bed and strolled around on the roof of the palace. And from the roof he saw a woman bathing—a very beautiful woman. **3**So David sent and inquired about the woman, and he was told, "This is Bathsheba, the daughter of Eliam and the wife of Uriah the Hittite."

4Then David sent messengers to get her, and when she came to him, he slept with her. (Now she had just purified herself from her uncleanness.) Then she returned home. **5**And the woman conceived and sent word to David, saying, "I am pregnant."

As you read the entire story in today's verses you will see that David tried to get Uriah to come home and have sex with Bathsheba, but his plan failed. So he pretty much had Uriah killed by placing him on the front lines of the war. He then married Bathsheba. He tried to cover up his sin by committing another huge sin.

It's just hard to read. Uriah was an honorable man. He served David with all he was. And he was betrayed by both David and his wife and ended up dead. Ouch. I wonder if Bathsheba could have ever imagined she would have found herself there. I'm certain she often looked back on that fateful day in the water and wished she had responded differently, even if it meant the King would be angry. Even if it meant her own death for denying him. I'm sure the thought crossed her mind.

The truth is that she mourned the loss of her husband. Whether or not she was a willing participant in what happened with the King, she grieved the loss of her husband. Her entire life changed in a moment's time. Her husband died, she was moved to a new home with new people and new responsibilities. And the loss of her husband was only the beginning of the consequences she would face as the result of her participation in David's huge mistake.

We have all had those times, I'm sure. We have all done things we wished we could take back. Perhaps they didn't end with the loss of someone we loved, but we regret them nonetheless. One thing we can learn from Bathsheba, whether she was a victim or a seductress, is that life does go on. We see it above and we will see it again in her story as we read more. Maybe today is the day you need to accept that life goes on. Maybe today you need to tell yourself that whatever happened to you...or whatever you did...it is no longer in charge of how you feel or how you live. Today you break the chains.

PRAY
Lord, that thing that happened, I don't want it to own me anymore. I don't want it to define me. Will you help me to repent, forgive and let go? Will you help me to see myself as who I am and not who I once was? In Jesus' name, amen.

JOURNAL
As you read the story of Bathsheba today take notes on the following journal page to record your initial thoughts.

Journal Page

_____

_____

_____

_____

_____

_____

_____

_____

_____

_____

_____

_____

_____

_____

_____

_____

_____

_____

_____

BATHSHEBA DAY TWO
DUST YOURSELF OFF

Was the story of Bathsheba as hard for you to read as it was for me? My heart hurt for her. And honestly, it doesn't matter to me if she was a willing participant in the situation or not. Well, I mean, if she wasn't then I feel even worse for her. My heart goes out to Bathsheba. First, she lost her husband, then life as she knew it. Let's read what happened next in 2 Samuel 12, starting at verse 13:

> **13**Then David said to Nathan, "I have sinned against the LORD."
>
> "The LORD has taken away your sin," Nathan replied. "You will not die. **14**Nevertheless, because by this deed you have shown utter contempt for the word of the LORD,*b* the son born to you will surely die."
>
> **15**After Nathan had gone home, the LORD struck the child that Uriah's wife had borne to David, and he became ill. **16**David pleaded with God for the boy. He fasted and went into his house and spent the night lying in sackcloth*c* on the ground. **17**The elders of his household stood beside him to help him up from the ground, but he was unwilling and would not eat anything with them.

18On the seventh day the child died. But David's servants were afraid to tell him that the child was dead, for they said, "Look, while the child was alive, we spoke to him, and he would not listen to us. So how can we tell him the child is dead? He may even harm himself."

19When David saw that his servants were whispering to each other, he perceived that the child was dead. So he asked his servants, "Is the child dead?" "He is dead," they replied.

20Then David got up from the ground, washed and anointed himself, changed his clothes, and went into the house of the LORD and worshiped. Then he went to his own house, and at his request they set food before him, and he ate.

21"What is this you have done?" his servants asked. "While the child was alive, you fasted and wept, but when he died, you got up and ate."

22David answered, "While the child was alive, I fasted and wept, for I said, 'Who knows? The LORD may be gracious to me and let him live.' **23**But now that he is dead, why should I fast? Can I bring him back again? I will go to him, but he will not return to me."

24Then David comforted his wife Bathsheba, and he went to her and lay with her. So she gave birth to a son, and they named him Solomon.

Now the LORD loved the child **25**and sent word through Nathan the prophet to name him Jedidiah because the LORD loved him.

When all was said and done David realized that he could do nothing to change the situation. It was beyond his control. All he could do at that point was move forward doing the right thing. So he let go of his regret, let go of his shame...he had already repented and asked God to forgive him...and he went to his wife and comforted her. He put himself aside and provided Bathsheba with what she needed at that time.

He couldn't change the past but he could certainly change the future. There's really not much written about Bathsheba's feelings or reactions to any of this. Other than the fact that she mourned and needed comfort. Yet the little we do find about her moving forward tells us she grew. She survived the unheard of and she didn't let it control who she became.

PRAY
Lord, can you help me to let go of my own regret? Can you help me to choose to allow my past to be the lessons I build my future on? Teach me how to

grow from the hurt and not allow it to negatively affect my future. In Jesus' name, amen.

BATHSHEBA DAY THREE
PAIN AS A SPRINGBOARD

Up to this point we can basically see Bathsheba as a victim. Everything that has happened so far has happened to her. She was "taken" by the King, her husband was killed, she was moved into the palace, and her child died. None of those things were her plan. It all happened as the result of someone else's behavior. Really, even this good thing we are about to look at was beyond her choice. But what she did with it was certainly her choice. At the close of 2 Samuel 12 we read the following:

> **24**Then David comforted his wife Bathsheba, and he went to her and lay with her. So she gave birth to a son, and they named him Solomon.

> Now the LORD loved the child **25**and sent word through Nathan the prophet to name him Jedidiah because the LORD loved him.

She finally had a child. She had a reason to get up every day. She had someone to pour herself into. She had purpose outside of the pain. She was a mother. Did you see who her son is? Solomon. As in King Solomon. As in the wisest man to ever live. SHE was his mother. SHE raised him. She taught him. She could have decided to just let him be. She could have allowed her grief to cut her off. But she didn't. She raised him and loved him. How do we know? There are two things that make it clear.

1. Many scholars believe that Bathsheba wrote Proverbs 31 for Solomon when he was preparing to marry the Pharaoh's daughter. They believe that Lemuel was indeed Solomon. She was the wise mother of the wisest King to ever live.
2. Solomon honored his mother. Look at 1 Kings 2:

    19So Bathsheba went to King Solomon to speak to him for Adonijah. The king stood up to greet her, bowed to her, and sat down on his throne. Then the king had a throne brought for his mother, who sat down at his right hand.

He stood to meet her, bowed down to her, and literally had a throne brought out for her so she could sit at his right hand. He honored his mother, because she was worthy of honor.

I can't help but think of the verse in Proverbs 31:28 that says "Her children rise up and call her blessed."

Bathsheba had been through a great deal of pain and suffering. She could have given up. She could have chosen to live in her past. But she chose to grieve, accept what she could not change, and become the woman she really wanted to be. She became THE Proverbs 31 woman. She helped to make Solomon who he was. I would venture to say that without the pain of her past she could not have taught Solomon all that she did.

So, while Bathsheba may have started out a victim, she grew into a victorious woman. Can you see areas of your own life that you can transition from victim to victorious? Can you see things you can make a step stool to help elevate you?

PRAY

Lord, I prayed yesterday that I don't want my past to control my future. But I also don't want those things to be forgotten. Would you show me to how to use them to help others? Would you show me how to turn them into strength and wisdom for my future and the future of others? In Jesus' name, amen.

FIVE

BATHSHEBA DAY FOUR
BECOMING ASSERTIVE

How does your heart feel about Bathsheba? Do you feel sorry for her? Do you judge her for her part in the story? Can you see her growing and developing before your eyes? It's a gradual growth, so it's not that easy to spot. But it's there. We looked at her journey into motherhood and how it changed her. As the death of King David approached it was easy to see how she had come into her own. Look at 1 Kings 1:

> **11**Then Nathan said to Bathsheba the mother of Solomon, "Have you not heard that Adonijah son of Haggith has become king, and our lord David does not know it? **12**Now please, come and let me advise you. Save your own life and the life of your son Solomon. **13**Go at once to King David and say, 'My lord the king, did you not swear to your maidservant, "Surely your son Solomon will reign after me, and he will sit on my throne"? Why then has Adonijah become king?' **14**Then, while you are still there speaking with the king, I will come in after you and confirm your words."
>
> **15**So Bathsheba went to see the king in his bedroom. Since the king was very old, Abishag the Shunammite was serving him. **16**And Bathsheba bowed down

in homage to the king, who asked, "What is your desire?"

17"My lord," she replied, "you yourself swore to your maidservant by the LORD your God: 'Surely your son Solomon will reign after me, and he will sit on my throne.' **18**But now, behold, Adonijah has become king, and you, my lord the king, did not know it. **19**And he has sacrificed an abundance of oxen, fattened calves, and sheep, and has invited all the other sons of the king, as well as Abiathar the priest and Joab the commander of the army. But he did not invite your servant Solomon. **20**And as for you, my lord the king, the eyes of all Israel are upon you to tell them who will sit on the throne of my lord the king after him. **21**Otherwise, when my lord the king rests with his fathers, I and my son Solomon will be counted as criminals."

I mentioned earlier in the week that most of what we read about Bathsheba had "happened to her". But no more. Bathsheba was not going to allow her son Solomon to be pushed aside. He would be King. She still had influence over King David, and she was going to use that. And she did. Adonijah was not a disciplined man. He was not chosen by God. But Solomon was. And Bathsheba was going to ensure that Solomon took his proper place. She was courageous, assertive and confident. A far cry from the Bathsheba at the start of this story.

David had promised her that Solomon would be king. 1 Kings tells us that Adonijah set himself up as king, without the blessing of his father, without the anointing of the prophet. He was arrogant and unrestrained. The prophet and the Queen ensured the rightful man would rule over Israel after David's death. And Bathsheba would be honored by her son, the king.

Maybe your life has been a series of things that happened to you. Maybe it started in childhood when you did not get what you needed from those who raised you. Perhaps it began later in a troubled relationship. Maybe you have not been strong enough to represent yourself according to who you are in Christ. That can change. That doesn't have to continue to be your story. You CAN be who God has called you to be. You really can. It will require you choosing. It will require you changing your mind and your words. But you can do it.

PRAY
Jesus, you died for my eternal salvation. But I know that you also died so that I could have life more abundant here on this earth. I don't want to get to heaven to find that I didn't receive all you had for me here. Would you begin to show me who I really am in you? I believe that the joy of the Lord is my strength, help me to be joyful and strong in You. In Jesus name, amen.

FIVE

BATHSHEBA DAY FIVE
CONSEQUENCES

This week has felt challenging to me. It felt less encouraging and more like a warning. But that's not a bad thing. Bathsheba's story didn't start out the best. There was pain and suffering. There was scandal and struggle. But she must have done something right along the way, as her son Solomon was the wisest man to ever live. He loved God and stayed close. But much like his father, it was women who were his downfall. Bathsheba saw it coming, long before it ever happened. Remember we talked about Proverbs 31? She warned her son before he married Pharaoh's daughter. But much like his father, he didn't listen until it was too late. Solomon bore the consequences of his choices. David and Bathsheba did too.

If found it strange that of the five women listed in the genealogy of Jesus, she was the only one not listed by name. In fact, she wasn't even listed as King David's wife. Take a look at Matthew 1:

> **1**This is the record of the genealogy of Jesus Christ, the son of David, the son of Abraham:
>
> **2**Abraham was the father of Isaac,
> Isaac the father of Jacob,
> and Jacob the father of Judah and his brothers.
>
> **3**Judah was the father of Perez and Zerah by Tamar,
> Perez the father of Hezron,

and Hezron the father of Ram.

4Ram was the father of Amminadab,
Amminadab the father of Nahshon,
and Nahshon the father of Salmon.

5Salmon was the father of Boaz by
Rahab,
Boaz the father of Obed by Ruth,
Obed the father of Jesse,
6and Jesse the father of David the
king,

David was the father of Solomon by
Uriah's wife,

Ouch. She was listed as Uriah's wife. I don't know
exactly why that is. But I can speculate. Will you
indulge me for a moment? I actually believe this is
a reminder that she never really was David's to
begin with. David was a man after God's own heart.
He loved God and God loved him. He was most
definitely close to God. But he sinned against God,
himself, Bathsheba, and Uriah. The consequence
of that sin stayed with him for the rest of his life. It
stayed with Bathsheba for the rest of her life too.
When I look at this statement in the list of Jesus'
ancestors I see a reminder that while Jesus throws
our sins as far as the east is from the west, our
consequences stay with us. So be careful what you
do. Be careful where you allow your mind to go.
Because where the mind goes the heart is sure to
follow.

As daughters of the King we are greatly blessed.
Jesus saved us. God has a great plan for our lives.

But that doesn't mean we get to live any way we want. The desire of our heart should be to please our Father. But how do we do that? We must be transformed by the renewing of our mind, just like the Bible tells us in Romans 12:2:

> Do not conform to the pattern of this world, but be transformed by the renewing of your mind. Then you will be able to test and approve what God's will is--his good, pleasing and perfect will.

How do we renew our mind? By reading the Bible and speaking it out of our mouth. Say the scriptures out loud. Pray them, write them down, repeatedly tell yourself what the Bible says about you. And while you are at it, be careful what else you put in there. If you are filling yourself with the Word AND garbage from the world...one is going to be pushed out. Paul told Timothy to guard his heart because out of it come the issues of life. Be cautious with what you are putting into your heart. More Word than World.

PRAY

Lord, I desire to live a life that is pleasing to You. I know that oftentimes that will mean I have to die to my own desires. I know that my spirit is more than willing to follow but that my flesh can be so weak at times. Help me to overcome my flesh and live by the spirit. Lead me, Lord. In Jesus name, amen.

JOURNAL

As we wrap up the week on Bathsheba, use the journal page to record your thoughts.

Journal Page

_____

_____

_____

_____

_____

_____

_____

_____

_____

_____

_____

_____

_____

_____

_____

_____

_____

_____

_____

_____

_____

_____

_____

Week Five - Mary
Simply Obedient

MARY DAY ONE
MY TAKE ON MARY

I often lead Bible studies about various women in the Bible. Of all of the studies I have done, I have only taught about Jesus' mother once. I think I just don't relate to her like I do some of the other women. Her story is far more neat and clean than mine. My story started out rocky and took years to get to where it is now. I relate to the woman with the alabaster box or any number of other far less perfect women. But for this particular study, I felt like God was asking me to include her. So, I did. It wasn't long after that I needed her story to speak to my heart and help me see clearly what God was trying to speak to me at the time. That story is the bonus content we will read later this week. But today, let's take a look at the story of Mary and how it all starts.

We first hear about Mary starting in Luke 1:26-38. She was a young girl. Some believe she was just thirteen years old. She was betrothed to a man named Joseph. In her culture that was as good as married. They had not yet consummated their marriage, but it was a done deal. So, when an angel visited Mary in this portion of scripture she was still a virgin, awaiting her wedding day. An angel showed up and spoke to her. As I read the story, it seemed to me that Mary was a pretty level headed lady...seemingly not as emotional as I am. Her responses were far less dramatic than mine would have been. The angel told Mary that she was going to carry the son of God. She asked him how that would be possible, since she was a virgin. The angel explained and Mary took him at his word.

Her response? "Be it unto me as you have said."

See! I would have been like, "Wait, wait, I need a little more information here." But not Mary. She obviously had a level of trust that I am only just now getting a glimpse of in my own life. Perhaps her early experiences helped her trust more than mine did. Whatever it was, she chose to obey what God was calling her to do, regardless of what that meant for her life.

We may look at what God was calling her to as an honor, and it was, but it was not going to be easy. Who would believe that she was still a virgin and was pregnant? No one. Why would they? And what about Joseph? He wasn't going to believe her either. Why would he? If he didn't believe her he could actually have her killed. Yes, killed. That was the law back then. But she didn't bat an eye.

Somehow, she knew that if God had chosen her to carry His son, sent an angel to tell her, and would place that baby in her womb, He would also protect her and work it all out. Somehow. She didn't ask Joseph if it was okay with him. She didn't run to her parents and ask their permission. She didn't talk to ten friends to see what they thought. She just said, "Yes, Lord." How is your "yes Lord"? Mine is broken sometimes. Mine is a little harder to get out of my mouth and into my heart.

As we read and study the story of Mary this week let's get a little introspective, let's ask ourselves if we respond to what God is asking of us as quickly or willingly as Mary did. Read Luke 1 and Mark 27 today and take notes on your thoughts and what God is speaking to you as you read.

PRAY
Lord, Jesus, I know you speak more often than I hear. Would you help me to settle myself and listen to what you are saying to me? And would you give me the courage to do what you ask? In Jesus name, amen.

READ
Luke Chapter 1 and Matthew chapter 27.

JOURNAL
As you read the story of Mary today take notes on the following journal page to record your initial thoughts.

Journal Page

_____

_____

_____

_____

_____

_____

_____

_____

_____

_____

_____

_____

_____

_____

_____

_____

_____

_____

MARY DAY TWO
CUT THE WORLD OUT

Yesterday, as you read the story of Mary, did it move you? Did you wonder how such a young girl could make such a huge commitment? I can only guess that Mary was close to God. She must have had family and leaders that pointed her toward Him all the time. In Luke 1:39, we see what Mary did immediately following her encounter with the angel.

> **39**In those days Mary got ready and hurried to a town in the hill country of Judah, **40**where she entered the home of Zechariah and greeted Elizabeth.
>
> **41**When Elizabeth heard Mary's greeting, the baby leaped in her womb, and Elizabeth was filled with the Holy Spirit. **42**In a loud voice she exclaimed, "Blessed are you among women, and blessed is the fruit of your womb! **43**And why am I so honored, that the mother of my Lord should come to me? **44**For as soon as the sound of your greeting reached my ears, the baby in my womb leaped for joy. **45**Blessed is she who has believed that the Lord's word to her will be fulfilled."

I don't know if she needed confirmation that what the angel said was true or if she knew Elizabeth would understand, but she went to visit her. And immediately Elizabeth confirmed that she would indeed be the mother of the savior of the world. Overwhelmed by the greatness and mercy of God Mary worshiped from her heart. And the first thing out of her mouth was, "My soul proclaims the greatness of the Lord".

She went on to pour out praises and glory to God, proclaiming who He is.

Then she stayed there, with Elizabeth for three months before returning home. Mary, although young, had great wisdom. She knew when to block out the noise of the world. She knew to go where she would be surrounded by faith and truth long enough to build herself up to face what was to come. Too often we run to all the wrong things and all the wrong people when we are trying to figure out what God is doing in our life. The truth is that if we would begin to tune in to God we could get the direction we so desperately need. Psalm 119:105 says that His Word is a lamp to our feet and light to our path. His Word. Not the advice of others. I mean, God will use other people to give us wisdom and insight - - the right people - - godly people. But their input and insight will often confirm what we already know deep inside. God speaks to us through His Word more than any other way. So in order to hear Him, we have to be in His Word.

Do you have a regular habit of reading the Word? If not, look at your schedule for the week and see if you can schedule a time each day to read the Bible and pray. It can be as little as 5 or 10 minutes. One verse, and a quick prayer. We have to start somewhere. You can work to expand it later. Just start by making time for Him.

FIVE

PRAY

Lord, I know I need to be closer to You. Will You remind me that I need to carve out some time in my day to read and pray and listen? Will you help me cut out the things that distract, so I can make the time for you that I so desperately need? And in that window of time, will You speak? In Jesus name, amen.

FIVE

MARY DAY THREE
LETTING GOD LEAD

As much as Mary trusted God, as much as she separated herself to cut out the noise, she must have still been nervous about what Joseph would say. She had to be concerned about his reaction. Any human being would be concerned for their own life. It's just how we are wired. As I mentioned earlier this week, in their culture a woman could be killed if found to have been unfaithful. Had Joseph made the news of her pregnancy public she could have been stoned to death. But that's not how the story went.

No, Joseph was a good man. He chose to, instead, quietly divorce Mary in order to protect her life. He obviously loved her, cared about her well-being. But God wanted Joseph to be Jesus' father. He wanted his influence in the natural life of this man who would grow up to save the world. So, once again, He sent an angel to intervene. Let's change books this time, and look at Matthew 1:18-24

> **18**This is how the birth of Jesus Christ came about: His mother Mary was pledged in marriage to Joseph, but before they came together, she was found to be with child through the Holy Spirit. **19**Because Joseph her husband was a righteous man and was unwilling to disgrace her publicly, he resolved to divorce her quietly.
>
> **20**But after he had pondered these

things, an angel of the Lord appeared to him in a dream and said, "Joseph, son of David, do not be afraid to embrace Mary as your wife, for the One conceived in her is from the Holy Spirit. **21**She will give birth to a Son, and you are to give Him the name Jesus,_d_ because He will save His people from their sins."

22All this took place to fulfill what the Lord had said through the prophet:

23"Behold, the virgin will be with child
and will give birth to a son,
and they will call Him Immanuel"
(which means, "God with us").

24When Joseph woke up, he did as the angel of the Lord had commanded him, and embraced Mary as his wife. **25**But he had no union with her until she gave birth to a Son. And he gave Him the name Jesus.

A handful of years ago God showed me something through this story of Mary. It helped me as a woman in ministry. It calmed my concerns and solidified my resolve to serve Him. I mentioned earlier that Mary and Joseph were betrothed. And that meant that they were legally bound in marriage even though they had not yet consummated that marriage. But as the angel presented Mary's calling to her she did not go to Joseph to ask permission to fulfill it. I know that statement will rub some people the wrong way, but before you freak out let me follow it up with this. She also didn't go to Joseph and say, "I'm doing this whether you like it or not". She didn't do anything. Well, she visited Elizabeth. But she didn't try to make her case. She simply waited. She said yes to God and trusted Him to make a way. She didn't fret, or plan a speech, or stand her ground. She just said yes and waited. And what happened? God revealed Himself to Joseph in a dream. He sent an angel to explain the situation so that he would surrender himself like Mary had done.

When God calls us, when He presents His plan for us, there is no need for us to fight for it. There is no need for us to shoulder our way through and make it happen. He will do it. He is God and we are not. So, ladies, are you concerned that you can't fulfill what God is calling you to do? Simply say yes, and wait. Pray and ask Him to make a way and light your steps when the time is right. He will. It may take 5 months, it may take 5 years. Trust Him. His timing is perfect. Always.

PRAY
Lord, I'm sorry for when I run ahead of You. And I'm sorry for when I quit in fear. I want to do what You want, when You want. I want to trust You to speak to whoever You need to in order to work out Your plan for my life. Help me to not try to help You. I trust You with my life. In Jesus name, amen.

FIVE

MARY DAY FOUR
REAL SURRENDER

I'm sure that surrendering as a young girl was difficult for Mary. But honestly, it was only training for the surrender that was yet to come. The real surrender would be in letting Jesus go. If you are a mom, or have a child in your life that you love and care about, you know how hard it would be to watch them die. But that is exactly what Mary was called to do. First, she was called to birth Him, the raise Him, then love Him through His own greatest and highest calling. To die for the world in place of us, for sins He never committed. John 19 tells us that she was right there at the cross:

> **25**Near the cross of Jesus stood His mother and her sister, as well as Mary the wife of Clopas and Mary Magdalene. **26**When Jesus saw His mother and the disciple whom He loved standing nearby, He said to His mother, "Woman, here is your son." **27**Then He said to the disciple, "Here is your mother." So from that hour, this disciple took her into his home.

Mary saw the crown of thorns on his head. The one twisted together by hands connected to twisted hearts bent on the destruction of not only our Savior, but her son. She saw the open wounds on his weak body. She saw the stream of blood that ran from the body she once carried within her own. She heard the sound of the nails piercing bones, and the cries of pain that forced their way from his deflated lungs. She heard his final words and saw his last breath escape his lifeless body. She felt every moment. She lived in the deepest places of despair in those moments, helpless and hopeless. No way out. She had been called to watch Him die. It took surrender. It was surrender that her entire life had prepared her for. In retrospect I'm sure she could see all of the times God had been stretching her, getting her ready. When Jesus stayed behind at the temple...and she was afraid for his life. When she called Him out to perform His first miracle. When He was accused and lied about. Every moment surely passed through her mind.

Surely, she had heard about his missing body. Her heart pounding loudly in her chest she must have questioned where He was. But in slow motion it all became clear. All the years, all the pain, all the surrender led her to that moment. And in that moment she saw the fulfillment of what God had called her to all those years before. When she was just a thirteen years old girl. When she couldn't have imagined all she would endure, all she would see with her tear stained eyes. She was obedient and faithful, and her purpose and His purpose had finally been fulfilled.

Can you allow yourself to see ahead into your future? Can you allow yourself to believe that everything will work together for good? That every joy, every struggle, every moment, will all come together for the finalization of your purpose in this life? It gets easier when we do. We can accept it all when we believe He is going to use it

PRAY

Dear Jesus, thank you for all that You endured for me. Thank you for loving me that much. I give you every moment of my life, Lord. Every struggle I have faced and have not understood, I hand it over and ask you to use it. Work it together with every other moment and make them glorify You, like only You can. In Jesus name, amen.

FIVE

MARY DAY FIVE
PURPOSE FULFILLED

We have come to not only the last day of the week, but the last day of the study. We end our time together on Mary. The mother of the Son of God. The one who carried Him in her own body, and then raised Him to be the man God called Him to be. She was obedient, faithful, and honorable. She gave him life on earth, and He gave her – and us - life in heaven. Mary, the final woman listed in the genealogy of Jesus. Let's take another look at that portion of scripture before we close.

Matthew 1:1-17

> **1**This is the record of the genealogy of Jesus Christ, the son of David, the son of Abraham:

> **2**Abraham was the father of Isaac,
> Isaac the father of Jacob,
> and Jacob the father of Judah and his brothers.

> **3**Judah was the father of Perez and Zerah by Tamar,
> Perez the father of Hezron,
> and Hezron the father of Ram.*a*

> **4**Ram was the father of Amminadab,
> Amminadab the father of Nahshon,
> and Nahshon the father of Salmon.

> **5**Salmon was the father of Boaz by Rahab,

Boaz the father of Obed by Ruth,
Obed the father of Jesse,
6and Jesse the father of David the
king.

Next:

David was the father of Solomon by
Uriah's wife,
7Solomon the father of Rehoboam,
Rehoboam the father of Abijah,
and Abijah the father of Asa._b_

8Asa was the father of Jehoshaphat,
Jehoshaphat the father of Joram,
and Joram the father of Uzziah.

9Uzziah was the father of Jotham,
Jotham the father of Ahaz,
and Ahaz the father of Hezekiah.

10Hezekiah was the father of
Manasseh,
Manasseh the father of Amon,_c_
Amon the father of Josiah,
11and Josiah the father of Jeconiah
and his brothers
at the time of the exile to Babylon.

12After the exile to Babylon:

Jeconiah was the father of Shealtiel,
Shealtiel the father of Zerubbabel,
13Zerubbabel the father of Abiud,
Abiud the father of Eliakim,
and Eliakim the father of Azor.

14Azor was the father of Zadok,
Zadok the father of Achim,
and Achim the father of Eliud.

15Eliud was the father of Eleazar,
Eleazar the father of Matthan,
Matthan the father of Jacob,
16and Jacob the father of Joseph,
the husband of Mary,
of whom was born Jesus, who is
called Christ.

17In all, then, there were fourteen
generations from Abraham to David,
fourteen from David to the exile to
Babylon, and fourteen from the exile
to the Christ.

I hope you didn't skip over it. I hope you really read
the names. Really connected with the fact that
these were actual people, who lived in the same
world we do. Yes, Forty-two generations of human
beings. Five women. A historical record of the
genealogy of Jesus Christ. From Abraham to Mary.
Normal everyday people. Normal everyday women.
They struggled with many of the same things we
do. Each one had something in common. They all
made a commitment to seek God, to follow, to
serve. Each one honored Him and each one was
honored. Named for all time in the history books of
our Savior's lineage.

I've said it before and I'll say it again. You are also
His descendant. You are his daughter. A joint heir
with Christ and a child of the living God. Every one
of these women served Him before Jesus died for

us. Their sins did not keep them from being used by God. How much more are you received? How far have your sins been thrown? He has a plan for you and your life. He has a desire to use you in His story. All you have to do is choose. Simply choose to say yes, like Mary did. With no worry about who or when or why. Just a simple, obedient yes.

Will you say yes today? Will you allow Him to have His way in your life? I promise you that what lies ahead with Him is far greater than anything you could think, hope or imagine. My heart pounds at the thought of what He will do with each one of you. When I was writing this devotion book I prayed for you. I prayed that this book would be a doorway you would use to step into a closer relationship with your Savior. Today is the day the door swings wide open. Step through.

PRAY
Holy Savior, I want to be all You have called me to be. Today I say yes. Today I choose to step through the door. I am Yours. Use my life. I choose to put aside worry and fear. I will not try to figure it out. I simply say yes and trust You to work it out. In Jesus name, amen.

JOURNAL
As we wrap up the week on Mary, use the journal page to record your thoughts. There is an extra journal page for additional thoughts as we close out our time together.

Journal Page

_____

_____

_____

_____

_____

_____

_____

_____

_____

_____

_____

_____

_____

_____

_____

_____

_____

_____

FIVE

ABOUT THE AUTHOR

Libbie Hall is an author, blogger and speaker. With more than twenty years in ministry, Libbie has mentored, coached and led people of all ages and backgrounds. She is the author of Hope Against Hope, Living your life so that no trial is wasted. She also published the devotional Daily Hope. She is married and has three children and two dogs. Libbie loves the beach, reading and coffee.

Made in the USA
Middletown, DE
23 February 2020